BACKYARD WILDLIFE

Bears

by Emily Green

BELLWETHER MEDIA · MINNEAPOLIS, MN

Note to Librarians, Teachers, and Parents:

Blastoff! Readers are carefully developed by literacy experts and combine standards-based content with developmentally appropriate text.

Level 1 provides the most support through repetition of high-frequency words, light text, predictable sentence patterns, and strong visual support.

Level 2 offers early readers a bit more challenge through varied simple sentences, increased text load, and less repetition of high-frequency words.

Level 3 advances early-fluent readers toward fluency through increased text and concept load, less reliance on visuals, longer sentences, and more literary language.

Level 4 builds reading stamina by providing more text per page, increased use of punctuation, greater variation in sentence patterns, and increasingly challenging vocabulary.

Level 5 encourages children to move from "learning to read" to "reading to learn" by providing even more text, varied writing styles, and less familiar topics.

Whichever book is right for your reader, Blastoff! Readers are the perfect books to build confidence and encourage a love of reading that will last a lifetime!

This edition first published in 2011 by Bellwether Media, Inc.

Library of Congress Cataloging-in-Publication Data
Green, Emily K., 1966–
  Bears / by Emily Green.
     p. cm. — (Blastoff! readers: Backyard wildlife)
  Includes bibliographical references and index.
  Summary: "Developed by literacy experts for students in kindergarten through grade three, this book introduces bears to young readers through leveled text and related photos"—Provided by publisher.
  ISBN 978-1-60014-437-0 (hardcover : alk. paper)
  1. Bears—Juvenile literature. I. Title.
  QL737.C27G7383 2010
  599.78—dc22
                                          2010006425

Printed in the United States of America, North Mankato, MN.

080110   1162

Contents

What Are Bears?   4

What Bears Can Do   6

What Bears Eat   14

Where Bears Live   18

Glossary   22

To Learn More   23

Index   24

Bears are large, furry animals. Most bears have black or brown fur.

Bears can stand up on their back legs. They can walk like people.

Bears have big paws. Their paws help them paddle through water.

paw

Bear paws have sharp **claws**. Claws help some bears climb trees.

Many bears rub their backs on trees. They leave their **scent** behind to keep other bears away.

Bears eat
berries, nuts,
grass, **insects**,
and meat.

Some bears eat honey. Some bears hunt for fish in water.

Most bears live
in forests. Bears
sometimes come
near towns or
homes to look
for food.

Bears **hibernate** in **dens** in the winter. They come out in spring to look for food. Time to hunt!

Glossary

claws—sharp, curved nails at the ends of an animal's fingers and toes

dens—caves or holes where bears hibernate

hibernate—to spend winter in a deep sleep

insects—small animals with six legs and hard outer bodies; insect bodies are divided into three parts.

scent—the smell of an animal

To Learn More

AT THE LIBRARY

Milton, Joyce. *Bears Are Curious*. New York, N.Y.: Random House, 1998.

Rockwell, Anne. *Backyard Bear*. New York, N.Y.: Walker & Company, 2006.

Simon, Seymour. *Wild Bears*. New York, N.Y.: SeaStar Books, 2002.

ON THE WEB

Learning more about bears is as easy as 1, 2, 3.

1. Go to www.factsurfer.com.

2. Enter "bears" into the search box.

3. Click the "Surf" button and you will see a list of related Web sites.

With factsurfer.com, finding more information is just a click away.

Index

berries, 14

claws, 10

climb, 10

dens, 20

fish, 16

food, 18, 20

forests, 18

fur, 4

grass, 14

hibernate, 20

homes, 18

honey, 16

hunt, 20

insects, 14

legs, 6

meat, 14

paddle, 8

paws, 8, 9, 10

people, 6

rub, 12

scent, 12

spring, 20

stand, 6

towns, 18

trees, 10, 12

water, 8, 16

winter, 20

The images in this book are reproduced through the courtesy of: Juan Martinez, front cover, p. 15 (right); David & Micha Sheldon/Photolibrary, p. 5; Ronald Wittek/Photolibrary, p. 7; Daniel J. Cox/KimballStock, p. 9; James Hager/Photolibrary, p. 11; Michael DeYoung/Photolibrary, p. 13; Bob Gurr/Photolibrary, p. 15; Geanina Bechea, p. 15 (left); Fong Kam Yee, p. 15 (middle); Eric LeFranc/Photolibrary, p. 17; Sergey Karpov, p. 19; C&C Bear Imagery/Photolibrary, p. 21.